"MAXI'S PRAYERS: A Family Legacy"

is the first book, in the Lunch Box Epistles series. Each epistle tells a story about God's amazing love and family values.

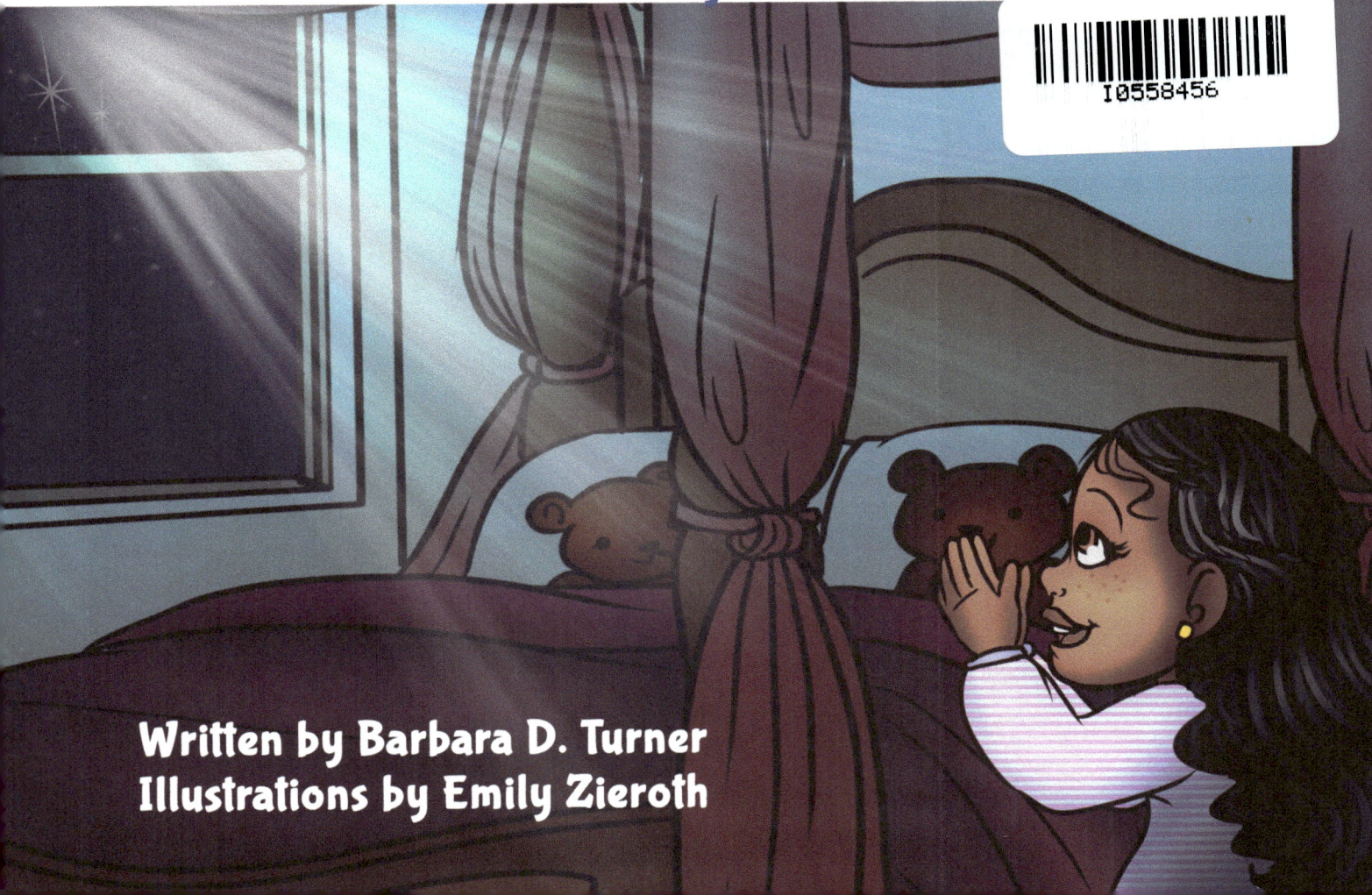

Written by Barbara D. Turner
Illustrations by Emily Zieroth

LUNCHBOX EPISTLES

MAXI'S PRAYERS: A Family Legacy
Part of the Lunchbox Epistles series

Copyright © 2021 by Barbara D. Turner

Cover Design and Book Illustrations by Emily Zieroth

LUNCHBOX EPISTLE Logo Design on page by ABI

DEDICATION

"MAXI'S PRAYERS: A Family Legacy" is dedicated to my nieces, nephews, Godchildren and sons and daughters in The Lord ...

Barbara D. Turner

ACKNOWLEDGEMENTS

A special note of thanks and appreciation to Pastor James Moore, Sr. and First Lady Reverend Margaret Moore, Rosetta Jamieson Thomas, Reverend Dr. Glenn E. Porter, Sr., Marissa Phifer, Shauna Jamieson Carty, Carla Wynter Darius, C. Jasey, and A.G. for sharing your editorial and literary gifts, as well as your encouragement, wisdom, love and prayer support with me, to help bring "MAXI 'S PRAYERS" to pass.

Barbara D. Turner

FOREWORD

When Barbara D. Turner asked me to write the "Foreword" of this maiden venture of the LunchBox Epistles, entitled "MAXI'S PRAYERS: A Family Legacy", I was humbled that I was given another opportunity to take part in another vehicle that promotes and fosters a closer relationship with Almighty God; especially as it relates to our communion with God through prayer.

There is a traditional adage often recited by elders and contemporaries of the African American Christian culture that is:
"PRAYER Is The Key—And Faith Unlocks The Door". For God's Word reminds us in Philippians 4:6–8{KJV}, "Be careful for nothing: but In everything by prayer and supplication with thanksgiving let your requests be made known unto God. And the peace of God, which passeth all understanding, shall keep your hearts and minds through Christ Jesus".

My prayer for the readers of this maiden venture, as well as the series of the "LunchBox Epistles" is that your hearts will be warmed and inclined to draw nearer and closer to Jesus Christ, as you embrace a more intimate relationship with Him through prayer.

Your Humble Servant In Jesus Christ, Pastor James E. Moore, Sr.
Second Baptist Church
Roselle, New Jersey 07203

Hi, my name is Maxine Marie Baxter. My Mommy and Daddy named me Maxine, after my Great-great-Grandmother; our name means great in French. They said I got my twinkly, brown eyes and cocoa brown skin from her and that Mathis, Melinda, and I were born to do great things for God, just like Great-great-Grandma Maxi.

Sunday was Great—great—Grandma Maxi's favorite day of the week. She loved going to church, singing in the choir, praying to God, and preparing a scrum—delicious meal for her family and friends to enjoy after service.

The church members or saints, as Daddy calls them, said that Great–great–Grandma Maxi was a "prayer warrior". She always said, "Prayer time is a special conversation between you and God."

I love going to Sunday School and church, so I can learn more about Jesus. Melinda, Mathis and I have a great time in the choir, dance ministry and youth group. Our friends do too.

I remember on Youth Sunday when Pastor Agee was preaching about prayer. He said, "Church when we pray, we are talking with God. And when God's people pray, AMAZING things can happen. The Bible says, in the Book of James, chapter 5, verse 16 that prayer is powerful, and prayer works. So, keep on praying! Our prayers can make a difference, they can change the world."

The whole church was clapping and saying, AMEN

*authors emphasis
with James 5:16 KJV

That night before I went to sleep, I was talking to God....

Dear God,

Thank you for helping me to learn more about prayer and spending this special time with You. Daddy and Mommy said, we were created to make a difference for You. Please let my prayers and words make a difference and help to change the world.

Our Grandad, Poppa B. tells us stories about Great-great-Grandma Maxi and many of our ancestors who were from Africa, Haiti and other countries around the world. His grandfather, Jeremiah Baxter told him the stories.

Generations

Poppa B. and our Nana,
Grandma Sophie, gave us a
big, beautiful scrapbook called:
Generations. It has lots of
pictures, stories, and family
history.

PAGE 2

RKET
RODUCTS

MISS EBONY'S SPECTACULAR PERFORMANCE

Lorem ipsum dolor sit amet, ex pro mundi vitae nostrum, his solet deserunt complectitur ei. Ei sit quodsi volutpat. Inani choro timeam ei vel, te his eros meliore. Quis lorem usu ut, no eam adhuc sonet, id qui congue consul temporibus. Sed ea essent patrioque. Eu pri utqui omnium docendi, vix ex putant accumsan petentium. Quo summo prodesset in, ex paulo tation gubergren vel.

Ex cum vocibus reprimique, nusquam moderatius mea cu. Est ea everti molestie aliquando, an sed dico nostro. Cu erant temporibus comprehensam vix, eum id impedit delenit adipisci. Nec eu commodo appetere posidonium, utamur singulis te pri, illum molestie tractato ex per. Eu his alienum voluptua. Te sit iusto putant, usu quem dico efficiantur ad. Usu ad nobis nonumy, sententiae temporibus pri an. Vim eu vocibus electram sapientem. Simul dicant elit ea.

Apeirian urbanitas an eum, pro no mets oratio, eam in nostro dolorem. Eu ius dico minimum, per ei diceret phaedrum. No sit altera quaerendum, postea posidonium ei qui. Ex eruditi saperet torquatos eum. Nam ne agam partiendo, te sit appetere percipitur. Mel ne fugit doctus nostrum. Eleifend inimicus adolescens mea ex. Veri dolorem theophrastus ea vix. Te sit iusto putant, usu quem dico efficiantur ad. Usu ad nobis nonumy, sententiae temporibus pri an. Vim eu vocibus electram sapientem. Simul ius dico minimum.

Poppa B. makes every story special; we go on adventures, learn words in other languages, sing songs, or look through our scrapbook. Sometimes we have a picnic under the stars, in my backyard listening to the stories and eating "yummy–to–my–tummy" food like fried chicken, collard greens, potato salad, mac & cheese, cornbread and chocolate cake.

Our family has lots of fun together. Game nights, Movie Marathons, The Baxter Family Cook—off, family trips to see our favorite teams play, celebrating birthdays, holidays, going to church, and keeping the family traditions.

We love going to my grandparents' house for Family Prayer Meetings. It is a Baxter tradition started by Great–great–Grandma Maxi. She said God gave her the idea to bring everybody together for a special time of prayer and fellowship.

Grandma Sophie sends beautiful invitations to our family and friends. They always smell like lemon verbena, her favorite perfume. We put our invitations in the scrapbook.

We set the tables with Grandma Sophie's gold cloths, fine china, and bouquets of roses from her garden. We also help make dinner. Melinda and I make homemade ice cream and put frosting on the cakes.

What a feast!

We have a grand time singing songs, clapping our hands, and listening to Poppa B. talk about Jesus. After service, we share family stories, lots of laughs, and our wonderful meal.

Later in the evening, Grandma Sophie gives us
sleeping bags and blankets so that we can stay
over. We play games and watch movies with our
cousins. Aunty Margorie always brings special
treats for the kids: Cotton candy, caramel popcorn,
chocolate chip cookies, or her good and gooey
brownies.

In the morning, the smell of pancakes, sausage, eggs, bacon and homemade biscuits fill the house. Mathis and I take our time eating the biscuits. We like to dip them in the butter and honey....

Before we go home, Poppa B. shares a story about one of our ancestors, we have prayer and he reminds us that God loves us and that we were created to do great things for Him.

THE END

MEET THE AUTHOR

As a young girl, Barbara was told about the love of Jesus Christ by her mother and grandfather, Mr. B. And it was with her grandfather that Barbara spent hours listening to radio broadcasts of her favorite MLB team and watching them on television. From those experiences, she developed a desire to " tell the story" and share the good news. God has given Barbara unique ways to share The Gospel of Jesus Christ through messages of love, empowerment, family values, social activism, and sports.

Maxi's Prayers: A Family Legacy is the first book in a series entitled: LunchBox Epistles. The epistles share messages of God's Amazing love with young people.